HARD NUTS
OF HISTORY

Travellers
and Explorers

TRACEY TURNER

ILLUSTRATED BY JAMIE LENMAN

A & C BLACK
AN IMPRINT OF BLOOMSBURY
LONDON   NEW DELHI   NEW YORK   SYDNEY

First published 2015 by A & C Black,
an imprint of Bloomsbury Publishing Plc
50 Bedford Square, London WC1B 3DP

www.bloomsbury.com

Bloomsbury is a registered trademark of Bloomsbury Publishing Plc

ISBN 978-1-4729-1095-0

A CIP catalogue for this book is available from the British Library.

Printed in China by Leo Paper Products, Heshan, Guangdong

1 3 5 7 9 10 8 6 4 2

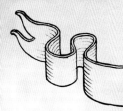

CONTENTS

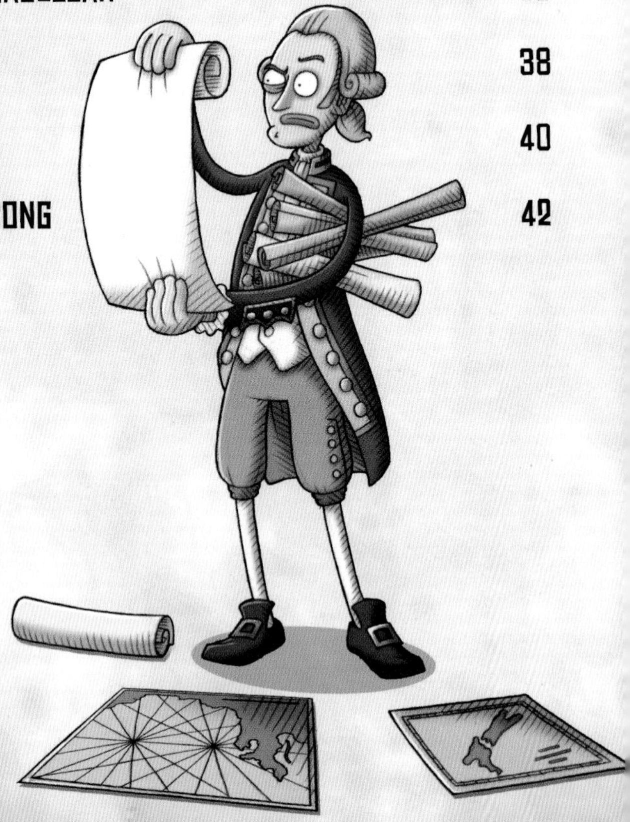

INTRODUCTION

This book contains the hardest and most courageous explorers and travellers in the history of the world. Some of them navigated uncharted waters, some braved the icy landscapes of the freezing Poles, and one even set foot on the surface of the Moon. But all of them were as hard as nails.

FIND OUT ABOUT . . .

- **The mysterious source of the White Nile**

- **The court of Kublai Khan**

- **The search for the Fountain of Youth**

- **Explorers' dreadful fates**

If you've ever wanted to cross the Rocky Mountains, besiege an Aztec city, or discover the Northwest Passage, read on. Follow the hard nuts through crocodile-infested swamps, across wind-blown wastelands, and into the vast emptiness of space.

As well as finding out about stories of discovery and courage, you might be in for a few surprises. Did you know, for example, that Walter Raleigh searched for a city made of gold? Or that Captain Cook was chopped to bits?

You're about to meet some of the toughest explorers who ever lived . . .

Plus turn to page 44 to find out what life is really like in space!

Plus turn to page 44 to find out what life is really like in space!

ROALD AMUNDSEN

Roald Amundsen was one of the toughest explorers of the lot, and became the greatest polar explorer ever.

A CHILLY EXPEDITION

Amundsen was born in 1872 in Norway and as soon as he was old enough he joined an expedition to the Antarctic. But the ship became trapped in Antarctic ice, and stayed that way for over a year. Almost everyone got scurvy, a horrible disease caused by a lack of vitamin C. Amundsen, being the tough nut that he was, took charge, organising everyone to catch penguins and seals for food, and make their skins into clothing and blankets. Eventually spring arrived and the ice melted – as much as it ever did in the Antarctic – and the expedition became the first ever to survive a whole winter there.

THE NORTH WEST PASSAGE

Amundsen wasn't put off by his icy experience. In 1903 he set off on his own expedition to find the North West Passage – a route connecting the Atlantic and Pacific that explorers had been seeking for hundreds of years. When he arrived at the Arctic, Amundsen learned from the tough-nut people who lived there about igloos and sledge-pulling dog teams. By 1906 he'd become the first person to navigate the North West Passage.

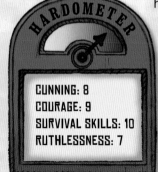

HARDOMETER

CUNNING: 8
COURAGE: 9
SURVIVAL SKILLS: 10
RUTHLESSNESS: 7

ANTARCTIC EXPEDITION

In 1911 Amundsen was back at the Antarctic, determined to reach the South Pole before Captain Scott's expedition (see page 52). He had four companions, four sledges and 52 dogs, and used his polar survival skills to combat the coldest temperatures on Earth, icy blizzards and perilous crevasses. He reached the South Pole on 14 December 1911, a month before Scott, by which time the team had eaten most of the dogs. Amundsen returned to Norway a hero, and was awarded a gold medal by the National Geographic Society in America.

POLE POSITION

Amundsen never stopped exploring. By the time he died in a plane crash in 1928, he'd become the first person to visit both Poles on foot and by air.

CHRISTOPHER COLUMBUS

Christopher Columbus discovered a whole New World – even though he wasn't really looking for it.

HOIST THE MAINSAILS!

Christopher Columbus was born in Italy in 1451 and first went to sea aged 14. He settled in Portugal, the sea-faring capital of the world at the time. He wanted to find a new sea route to Asia, which he hoped would make him rich, and have a fantastic adventure at the same time. He came up with the new and exciting idea of getting there by sailing west (like most educated people of the time, he knew the world was round).

I'VE FOUND INDIA!

LAND AHOY!

Columbus needed funds and ships. No one in Portugal would help him, but King Ferdinand and Queen Isabella of Spain liked his ideas and so gave him the money to fund his expedition. In 1492 he set sail in three ships, and by October he had reached the Caribbean. Columbus thought he'd reached Asia, so he called the locals 'Indians'. He travelled on to Cuba and Hispaniola (modern-day Haiti and the Dominican Republic), where he built a fort from the wreck of one of the ships and left some of his men. Then he sailed back to Spain, his ships full of exotic plants, gold, parrots and a few of the friendly local people, and announced that he'd discovered the West Indies.

ROUGH SEAS

Columbus sailed on two more voyages, and explored the Caribbean coast of South America. On the second of the two, he got into trouble: the people who'd been left at the fort on Hispaniola had been killed by the locals, and Columbus was accused of managing things badly. He'd also made the mistake of not finding any gold. He returned to Spain a prisoner on one of his own ships.

FINAL VOYAGE

Columbus persuaded the Spanish to send him on another Atlantic voyage in 1504, but his ships were wrecked on the Jamaican coast and he had to be rescued. He died a year and a half later, without ever knowing that he hadn't sailed to Asia after all. He never set foot on the North American mainland, but his discovery of the New World changed the world forever.

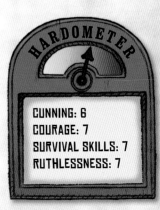

HARDOMETER

CUNNING: 6
COURAGE: 7
SURVIVAL SKILLS: 7
RUTHLESSNESS: 7

THE NEW WORLD

More explorers followed Christopher Columbus across the Atlantic Ocean from Europe. In the 1500s, the world they knew consisted of Europe, Africa and Asia – the Old World. Now they discovered North and South America – the New World.

NATIVES OF THE NEW WORLD

The people of the New World were in for a big surprise, and it wasn't a nice one. When the Europeans arrived they claimed land for their own countries, without bothering to ask if it already belonged to anyone. Columbus was very keen on the idea of enslaving as many Native Americans as possible. Hundreds of thousands of them were enslaved, killed in battles with the Europeans, or died from diseases that they'd never come into contact with before, brought over by the invaders. The native people of some parts of the New World died out completely, and it's been estimated that around a hundred million Native American people died. Amazingly, there are still some Native Americans, deep in the rainforest of the Amazon, who have never come into contact with Europeans to this day.

RICH EUROPEANS

Once they'd dealt with the people who lived there, the European invaders could get on with exploiting the New World and making themselves rich. Gold, silver and other precious metals were found in South America, and are still mined there today. Vast expanses of fertile land could be used to grow crops such as sugar, which fed the Europeans' increasing appetite for sweet treats. More and more Europeans left their own crowded countries to settle in the New World.

NEW WORLD FOOD

Chocolate, made from the beans of the cacao tree native to Central and South America, was made into a bitter drink by the Aztecs. A sweetened version became fashionable all over Europe, though chocolate wasn't eaten until the 19th century. The Old World also got its first taste of tomatoes, sweetcorn, turkey, vanilla, pineapples and potatoes from the New World.

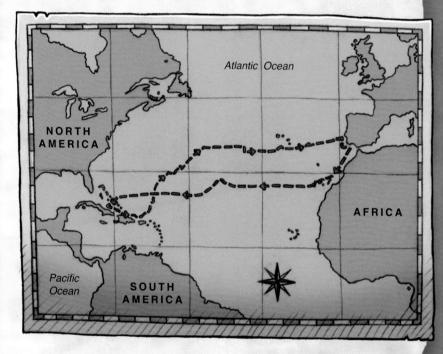

This map shows the first route Christopher Columbus took to the New World. He sailed on three more voyages after this.

AMELIA EARHART

Defying the conventions of her time, Amelia Earhart was a pioneering aviator, and became the first woman to fly solo across the Atlantic and Pacific Oceans.

HARD NUT RATING: 7

FIRST FLIGHT

Amelia Earhart had worked as a nurse and a social worker before she first flew in a plane in 1920, at the age of 23. The flight appealed to her sense of adventure, and within a week she was taking flying lessons. Six months later she had saved up enough money to buy her first plane. She flew the bright yellow plane, nicknamed Canary, to 14,000 feet, setting her first women's world record.

ATLANTIC FLIGHT

The race was on to be the first female pilot to cross the Atlantic. Earhart managed it in 1928, flying with two male pilots from Newfoundland to Wales in a journey that took 21 hours. Flying in the 1920s was much more dangerous than it is today and sadly three women had already died in 1928 in attempts to set the record.

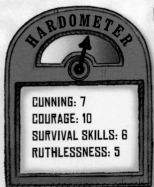

HARDOMETER

CUNNING: 7
COURAGE: 10
SURVIVAL SKILLS: 6
RUTHLESSNESS: 5

GOING SOLO

Earhart planned her next daring expedition: a solo flight across the Atlantic. She set off from Newfoundland in 1932 on a flight plagued with gales, freezing temperatures and mechanical problems. She was heading for Paris, but made an emergency landing in a field in Ireland. But she'd made it across the Atlantic – and was awarded a Distinguished Flying Cross, the first ever given to a woman. She said the flight proved men and women were equal in "intelligence, coordination, speed, coolness and willpower". In 1935, Earhart became the first woman to fly solo across the Pacific, from Honolulu to California.

AROUND THE WORLD

Earhart wanted to become the first woman to fly around the world, a journey of over 46,600 kilometres. She set off from Florida in 1937, and in less than a month she and her co-pilot, Fred Noonan, had covered over 35,400 kilometres. For the final leg of the journey, from New Guinea to Howland Island in the middle of the Pacific, they threw anything that wasn't absolutely necessary out of the plane to make room for extra fuel. But they never reached their destination. No one knows what happened, but Earhart and Noonan probably ran out of fuel, and died at sea.

FEMALE EXPLORERS

As well as having to contend with shark-infested seas, angry leopards and Pacific gales, women explorers have had to battle against the conventions of society, which expected them to get on with their embroidery in between looking after their children and husbands. And that was just the rich women – poor women had even less choice. Here are a three more truly tough women, who defied convention to become explorers.

ISABELLE EBERHARDT

Eberhardt was born in Switzerland in 1877. She first travelled to North Africa with her mother when she was 20, and after both her parents died she spent most of the rest of her life in Africa. She often dressed as a man to get around the strict rules for women, and did her best to help the poor and fight injustice. She sometimes got into trouble: in 1901 a man attacked her with a sabre and almost cut her arm off, but Eberhardt forgave him and pleaded for his life when he was sentenced to death (she succeeded). Her life was cut short when she died in a flash flood in Algeria in 1904.

ISABELLA BIRD

Born in England in 1831, Isabella Bird was 41 before she finally achieved her exploring ambitions. But she made up for lost time: she visited Australia, Hawaii (where she climbed volcanoes) and the Rocky mountains, which she explored in the company of a notorious outlaw. She made other expeditions to Japan, Vietnam, Singapore, Malaysia, India, Turkey, Kurdistan, Iran, and finally China. She was planning another trip to China when she died, aged 72.

ALEXANDRINE TINNÉ

Tinné was born in 1835 in the Netherlands. After her rich father died when Tinné was ten, she and her mother used their great wealth to travel around Europe, the Middle East and Egypt. They explored the course of the White Nile and the Sudan, and were hoping to explore the lakes of central Africa, but both Tinné's mother and aunt died of fever. Tinné decided to carry on exploring. She was crossing the Sahara Desert in the company of Tuareg nomads in 1869 when she was murdered – possibly because her water tanks were rumoured to be filled with gold.

ISABELLA BIRD

BURKE AND WILLS

Robert Burke and William Wills led an expedition across Australia, but never made it back.

HARD NUT RATING: 6.3

A BAD BEGINNING

Robert Burke, a police superintendent with no exploring experience, was appointed to lead an expedition across the unexplored middle of Australia from north to south, with William Wills as his second-in-command. In August 1860 they set off from Melbourne with a team of 22 men, plus horses, camels and wagons. It took them two months to reach Menindee, although the mail coach regularly made the journey in just over a week. Burke knew that there was a reward for the first north-south trip, and he knew there was a rival expedition, so he and Wills went on with a smaller group, desperate to win.

SWAMPLAND

At Cooper's Creek in Queensland, the group split again. Burke carried on with Wills and two other men, Gray and King, in the sizzling heat of the Australian summer, leaving the others to wait. Sick and exhausted, the small group staggered on. Burke and Wills travelled the final 24 kilometres on their own and came within sight of the northern coast of Australia, but didn't quite make it all the way because of crocodile-infested swamps. The two men met up with Gray and King, and began the rain-soaked journey back to Cooper's Creek and the rest of the team. They were tired, sick

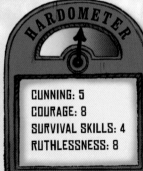

HARDOMETER

CUNNING: 5
COURAGE: 8
SURVIVAL SKILLS: 4
RUTHLESSNESS: 8

and low on supplies, so they ate their exhausted animals, plus a large snake discovered by Gray.

A HOPELESS JOURNEY

Gray died, and when the remaining three men arrived at Cooper's Creek they discovered that everyone else had left only hours before. Burke set out for the appropriately named Mount Hopeless, but returned to Cooper's Creek when the last two camels died. The three men were on their way to an Aboriginal camp to ask for help when Burke and Wills both died. The only survivor of their small team was tough-nut John King, who was helped by the Aborigines. Burke and Wills did become the first non-Aboriginal people to cross the continent, but didn't live to receive the prize money.

19

CAPTAIN COOK

HARD NUT RATING: 8.3

Captain James Cook discovered and named hundreds of islands and coasts, sailed all the world's oceans and twice around the world.

UNCHARTED TERRITORY

James Cook was a lieutenant in the British Royal Navy, and a skilled and experienced sailor, when he was chosen to captain a voyage of discovery to the Pacific in 1768. His crew included astronomers to observe the planets, and botanists to record the plants and animals they found. After a stay in Tahiti, Cook searched for the fabled but unmapped 'southern continent'. He found New Zealand instead, and mapped both the North and South Islands of the country. He sailed west to the east coast of Australia, which he mapped and promptly claimed for Britain, naming it New South Wales. He returned from the voyage having mapped 8,000 kilometres of previously uncharted territory.

THE SOUTHERN CONTINENT

Cook had been so successful on his first trip that he was soon off again. In 1772 he sailed with two ships, determined to find the southern continent he'd searched for on his first voyage. In 1773, he came closer to the South Pole than anyone before him, but just missed Antarctica.

HARDOMETER

CUNNING: 8
COURAGE: 9
SURVIVAL SKILLS: 8
RUTHLESSNESS: 8

THE NORTHWEST PASSAGE

By this time, Cook was famous and he could have weighed anchor for good, but he couldn't resist the quest for the Northwest Passage (a shortcut linking the Atlantic and Pacific). He didn't find it, but instead spent six months mapping the northwest coast of North America, and discovering the Hawaiian Islands. He got on well with the Hawaiians at first, but things took a turn for the worse.

COOK'S HORRIBLE END

Cook outstayed his welcome with the Hawaiians, and ended up being attacked and killed by them, along with ten of his men. The bodies were cut up and shared among the Hawaiian chiefs. The crew asked for Cook's body to be returned to them, and finally gruesome packages began to arrive – bits of burnt bones with some flesh left on them, and various body parts. Finally Cook's remains were buried at sea.

EXPLORING AUSTRALIA

Dutch explorer, Willem Janszoon, was the first European to land in Australia, crossing the Pacific from the islands of Indonesia in 1606. Captain Cook (see page 20) was the first to explore the east coast of Australia, in 1770. Not long after that, the British began to colonise the huge Australian continent.

HARD CORE EXPLORERS

EDWARD EYRE

At the end of the 1700s, the new colonists knew a bit about some of the Australian coast, but not much about the rest of the country – and there was an awful lot of it. Intrepid explorers set off on expeditions, battling barren deserts, humid rainforests, tall mountains, and some of the world's most dangerous wildlife. Some expeditions were just a team of two or three, while others included Aborigine guides, skilled craftsmen, horses, camels and other animals, as well as the expedition leaders. Here are a few of them:

- John Stuart, who was in competition with Burke and Wills (see page 18) to cross Australia from south to north, managed it in 1862. His route crossed the arid centre of Australia.

- Edward Eyre and his friend Wylie, an Aborigine, set off as part of a team to cross Southern Australia from west to east, a journey that took them across the hot, dry Nullarbor Plain. Their expedition quickly became a desperate search for water, and they were helped to find it by other Aborigines, who taught them to suck gumtree roots and recognise native wells.

- Ludwig Leichhardt travelled from Sydney, on the east coast, to Port Essington, near Darwin in the north of Australia – 5,000 kilometres of perilous country, which he covered in 18 months. Two years later he set off on an attempt to travel from Brisbane in the east to Perth in the west, across the centre of Australia, but he and his team disappeared. No trace of them has ever been found.

HARD NUT ABORIGINES

The Aborigines had been living in Australia for thousands of years before the European colonists turned up. Many of them died from diseases brought to Australia by Europeans, especially smallpox and tuberculosis. Their land was taken from them, and they weren't given the same rights as the settlers.

WYLIE

HERNÁN CORTÉS

HARD NUT RATING: 8.8

Cortés was a Spanish Conquistador (conqueror), who crossed the Atlantic to conquer the Aztecs of Central America.

ADVENTURES IN THE NEW WORLD

Hernán Cortés studied law at university, but gave it up for a life of adventure. In 1504 he sailed for the island of Hispaniola (now Haiti and the Dominican Republic), and then to Cuba, where he helped hard nut conqueror Diego Velasquez conquer the island, and gained a reputation for ruthlessness and courage in the process. In 1518, Cortés took charge of an expedition to Mexico, which had only recently been discovered by Europeans.

AZTEC EMPEROR

When Cortés got to Mexico, his men didn't seem too keen on staying. So in true hard-nut style he sank the ships they'd arrived in – now the conquest had to succeed. Cortés headed for the beautiful capital city of the mighty Aztec empire, Tenochtitlan. He was welcomed by the Aztec emperor, Montezuma II, who thought Cortés was the prophesied god Quetzalcoatl. Rather rudely, Cortés imprisoned Montezuma and demanded a huge ransom for his release.

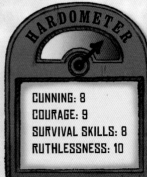

HARDOMETER

CUNNING: 8
COURAGE: 9
SURVIVAL SKILLS: 8
RUTHLESSNESS: 10

REVOLTING AZTECS

Jealous of Cortés, Velazquez sailed to Mexico for a punch-up. Cortés left Tenochtitlan to deal with Velazquez, but while he was away there was an Aztec revolt. When he returned, he found Montezuma had been killed in the mayhem, and the Spanish had been driven out of the city by angry Aztecs. Cortés besieged Tenochtitlan for three months, starving the Aztecs to death. When the city fell, Cortés destroyed it and built Mexico City on its ruins. Ruthless Cortés showed no mercy to the Aztecs and other indigenous people – lots of them were killed, or died of diseases the Europeans brought with them.

EXPLORING CALIFORNIA

Cortés was made governor of the old Aztec empire. But the Spanish thought he was getting a bit too powerful, and sent him back to Spain and reduced his powers. Cortés returned to Central America and carried on exploring, hoping to find a sea route between the Atlantic and the Pacific. He was disappointed, but cheered up when he discovered California instead. He finally returned to Spain in 1541, where he died six years later.

BURTON AND SPEKE

HARD NUT RATING: 7.3

Victorian explorers Burton and Speke searched for the source of the River Nile in Africa, and one of them found it.

THE SOURCE OF THE NILE

The Blue Nile joins the White Nile to form the River Nile that flows through Egypt. The Blue Nile's source had been discovered in the mountains of Ethiopia, but the source of the White Nile was a mystery. English explorers Richard Burton and John Speke set off to discover the mysterious source in 1857.

POORLY EXPLORERS

Burton had injured his legs, Speke had an eye problem and an ear infection, and both men were suffering from malaria, so they had to be carried by porters. Speke's ear infection was especially gruesome: a beetle had crawled into his ear one night and foolishly he'd tried to get it out using a penknife, badly damaging his ear. Despite all this, Burton and Speke became the first Europeans to explore Lake Tanganyika. Burton was too sick to continue, but Speke went on without him to look for a great lake that some traders had described. Further north he found it, and renamed it Lake Victoria after the British Queen.

BURTON GETS CROSS

Burton was absolutely furious that Speke had discovered the lake without him – especially if it was the source of the White Nile as Speke claimed – and the pair had an enormous row. Speke returned to England ahead of Burton, claimed all the credit and made the expedition famous. Burton was livid, especially when Speke was sent back to

Lake Victoria on his own. When Speke returned, he said that Lake Victoria definitely was the source of the Nile, but he hadn't done much about proving it. Burton said he was talking nonsense.

A HEATED DEBATE

In 1864 the two men were due to have a public debate about the source of the Nile, but Speke shot and killed himself while he was hunting the day before – no one's sure whether he'd meant to kill himself. Although he hadn't proved it, Speke was right about Lake Victoria: Henry Stanley (see page 35) confirmed it was the source of the Nile a few years later.

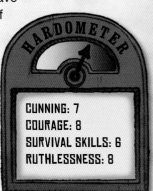

HARDOMETER

CUNNING: 7
COURAGE: 8
SURVIVAL SKILLS: 6
RUTHLESSNESS: 8

LEIF ERICSON

Nearly 500 years before Columbus, hard nut Viking Leif Ericson had already sailed across the Atlantic to North America.

HARD NUT RATING: 8.5

WESTERN LAND

Ericson was born around 970 AD in Iceland, then moved to Greenland after his father, Eric the Red, was exiled. In Greenland, Ericson heard the story of an Icelandic trader called Bjarni Herjólfsson, who said he'd been blown off course between Iceland and Greenland, and spotted land to the west full of thick forests and green hills. Ericson was keen for adventure, and planned his own expedition.

LEIF SETS SAIL

Round about 1000 AD, Ericson sailed his Viking longship with a crew of 35 in search of the new land. He didn't have a map, or even a compass, but followed Herjólfsson's description as best he could. He stopped off in places he called Helluland – probably Baffin Island – and Markland – probably Labrador. Battling through howling gales, fierce currents, and navigating around icebergs, Ericson was determined to keep sailing until he found the land of forests Herjólfsson had seen. The sailors rowed the Viking ship for days on end, living on porridge and dried fish and meat.

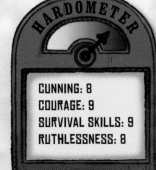

HARDOMETER

CUNNING: 8
COURAGE: 9
SURVIVAL SKILLS: 9
RUTHLESSNESS: 8

VIKING VINLAND

Eventually, Ericson did find the new western land. He landed in Newfoundland, a big island off the coast of Canada, and called it Vinland. Ericson and his crew built houses along the mouth of a river and stayed for the winter. Around a thousand years later, in the 1960s, an archaeological dig in northern Newfoundland discovered a Viking settlement that fitted the description of Vinland.

RETURN TO VINLAND

Leif returned to Greenland with stories of trees (which were in short supply in Iceland and Greenland), fruits, and rivers teeming with fish. A group of a hundred or so Greenlanders set off for the new land, but the Indians who already lived there didn't make them very welcome, and they came back. Even though he didn't stay, Leif Ericson is famous as the first European ever to set foot on North American soil.

VINLAND

LEWIS AND CLARK

Lewis and Clark became the first US settlers to travel across the vast North American continent.

HARD NUT RATING: 7.8

MOUNTAINS AND MAMMOTHS

In 1803 President Thomas Jefferson sent Meriwether Lewis and William Clark to find a route along the Missouri River and over the Rocky Mountains to the Pacific Ocean. Their mission was to explore the uncharted west, laying claim to land and establishing trade with Indians along the way. Jefferson thought they would find volcanoes, woolly mammoths and mountains of salt.

FROZEN RIVER

Lewis, Clark and their team set off in three boats from St Louis in the Midwestern United States. The Missouri River took them north into what's now North Dakota, where they spent their first winter because the river was completely frozen. They hired a French-Canadian fur trapper, and his wife Sacagawea, an Indian from the Shoshone tribe who turned out to be very helpful. Sacagawea helped with the explorers' route and negotiations with Indian tribes, found edible plants and made clothes and shoes. One Indian chief they ran into turned out to be her brother.

BEARS AND BLIZZARDS

When the ice melted in spring, the explorers entered territory where no settler had ever set foot. Their journey took them across the Rocky Mountains, over the Great Falls, through sandstorms, blizzards and three-metre-deep snow, all the way to the Pacific Ocean. On the way they encountered grizzly bears and different Indian tribes: some were friendly and others weren't.

TRIUMPHANT RETURN

On the way back, Lewis and Clark split up for part of the journey. When they met again, one of Clark's team mistook Lewis for an elk and shot him through the thigh. But Lewis was tough enough to limp back to St Louis, and the pair became the first Europeans to cross the huge continent of North America, arriving two years, four months and ten days after they'd set off. By that time, everyone had presumed them dead, and they were welcomed as heroes.

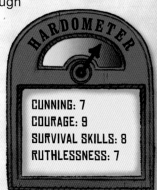

HARDOMETER

CUNNING: 7
COURAGE: 9
SURVIVAL SKILLS: 8
RUTHLESSNESS: 7

DREADFUL DISEASES

Explorers had to be hard enough to set off into unknown territory – they might find treacherous seas, arid deserts, freezing temperatures, or dangerous animals. But that wasn't all – diseases were out to get them too . . .

SCURVY

Scurvy has an unpleasant list of symptoms – aches and pains, tiredness, pale, blotchy and bruised skin, swollen limbs, spongy, bleeding gums and loose teeth – and if it's left untreated it's deadly. It's caused by a lack of vitamin C, found in fresh fruit and vegetables. In the 1740s, British navy doctor James Lind proved that eating lemons and limes could cure scurvy, and Captain Cook (see page 20) gave his crew pickled cabbage to ward off the disease. However doctors became convinced that the disease was caused by something else, and the disease plagued polar expeditions, such as Scott's (see page 52), into the 20th century.

MALARIA

Malaria is caused by a tiny parasite that gets into the bloodstream via a mosquito bite. Since there are a lot of malaria-carrying mosquitoes, especially in Africa, explorers were often exposed to this horrible disease (Livingstone, Burton and Speke all suffered from it – see pages 34 and 26). Malaria sufferers have flu-like symptoms, as well as diarrhoea and vomiting, and the disease can kill. Malaria isn't the only deadly disease caused by mosquitoes. They can also carry yellow fever and dengue fever.

GANGRENE

In the days before antibiotics (which weren't discovered until the 20th century), infected wounds were very difficult to treat, and badly infected wounds could lead to gangrene. If gangrene sets in, the skin turns dark green or black, the flesh starts to rot, and the wound absolutely stinks. If the injured part of the body isn't amputated, the sufferer can die.

As well as these deadly diseases, explorers might suffer from all sorts of other horrible conditions caused by bad food, dirty water, freezing temperatures and assorted germs.

JAMES LIND

DAVID LIVINGSTONE

Livingstone was a doctor and a missionary who explored Africa, and ended up losing his heart there.

HARD NUT
RATING: 7.5

LIVINGSTONE'S MISSION

David Livingstone was born in 1813 into a fairly poor Scottish family, and started work in the local mill at the age of ten. He saved money, went to university to study medicine, and became a missionary – someone who went to foreign countries hoping to convert people to Christianity.

MISSION IMPOSSIBLE

In 1840 Livingstone arrived at his post at the edge of the Kalahari Desert in southern Africa. But he quickly became more interested in exploring than in converting people to Christianity – in fact it's thought he only managed to convert *one* person the whole time he was there! He explored the region around the Zambesi River, searched for the source of the Nile (like Burton and Speke, see page 26), named Victoria Falls on the Zambesi, and became the first European to cross Southern Africa.

HARDOMETER

CUNNING: 6
COURAGE: 10
SURVIVAL SKILLS: 9
RUTHLESSNESS: 5

While he was busy exploring, Livingstone used his medical knowledge to help people, and he was especially good at treating malaria, a disease that still kills millions of people today. He also campaigned against slavery, which was illegal in Britain but was still going on in Africa.

LOOKING FOR LIVINGSTONE

In Britain, Livingstone had become a celebrity, but he only returned twice. When there was no word from him for years, everyone wondered what had happened to him. An American newspaper sent journalist Henry Stanley to find him – it took him eight months, but Stanley found Livingstone living in a remote African village. He greeted him with the famous words 'Dr Livingstone, I presume?' and gave him all the letters that had been piling up for him while no one knew where he was.

LIVINGSTONE'S LAST JOURNEY

Livingstone stayed in Africa. When he died, in 1873, his African friends dried out his body and carried it 1,500 kilometres to the coast, where it was shipped to England and buried in Westminster Abbey. But his heart was buried in Africa.

FERDINAND MAGELLAN

Magellan was a Portuguese explorer who led the first expedition to sail all the way around the world.

EXPLORING AND CONQUERING

Ferdinand Magellan was 12 years old when Columbus (see page 10) discovered a New World on the other side of the Atlantic. He went to sea with the Portuguese fleet, which sailed east and conquered Malacca (in what's now Malaysia), and explored the Spice Islands, in what's now Indonesia. He was also the first European to note the Magellanic Penguin!

WESTWARD EXPEDITION

Magellan proposed an expedition to find a westward route to the Spice Islands. The King of Portugal refused to fund it, so Magellan stormed off to Spain in a huff, where the Spanish King Carlos I gave him five ships for his expedition.

In 1519 Magellan set sail across the Atlantic with a crew of around 250, hoping to find a route through Brazil to the Pacific. He didn't find one, for obvious reasons.

MUTINY AND SHIPWRECK!

Some of the sailors were fed up with Magellan's expedition, and mutinied. Magellan restored order by executing and marooning some of the men, but two ships were lost: one was wrecked on a reef, and another mutinied and escaped back to Spain. Finally, Magellan got on with the business of sailing around the world, and found a passage west around the tip of South America, sailing past snow-capped mountains and the archipelago of Tierra del Fuego in rough seas.

FATAL FIGHT

Since he was the first European ever to cross it, Magellan had no idea that the Pacific Ocean is extremely big. The expedition spent months without sight of land. With few provisions and hardly any fresh food, many of the crew died of starvation or scurvy. But eventually they did find the islands now called the Philippines. Unfortunately, Magellan didn't make himself very popular with the Philippine islanders: there was a battle, during which Magellan was set upon by islanders and hacked to bits.

THE EXPEDITION CONTINUES

Magellan was dead, but the expedition wasn't over. Two of the ships eventually returned to Spain, having successfully circumnavigated the world – the first ever to sail around the world.

HARDOMETER

CUNNING: 8
COURAGE: 9
SURVIVAL SKILLS: 6
RUTHLESSNESS: 10

MARCO POLO

Marco Polo was an Italian explorer who gave medieval Europe its first taste of Asia.

HARD NUT
RATING: 7.8

A LONG JOURNEY

Marco Polo's father and uncle were jewel merchants from Venice, and travelled all the way to China to trade their jewels. When Marco Polo was 17, he went with them on a trip to China, sailing across the Mediterranean to Acre (now in Israel) then thousands of kilometres by land across Asia to Shandu, and the court of the Mongol ruler of China, Kublai Khan. The journey took three and a half years.

THE COURT OF KUBLAI KHAN

Kublai Khan, Genghis Khan's grandson and ruler of the second biggest empire in the history of the world, was very impressed with Marco Polo. He was so impressed that he made him a diplomat, and then governor of the city of Yangzhou. After 17 years at Kublai Khan's court, the Polos decided it was time to go home, but the emperor was very reluctant to let them leave.

HEADING HOME

In 1292, Marco Polo and his father and uncle set sail from south China and began their journey home. Kublai Khan had asked them to escort a Mongol princess to Persia (modern-day Iran), and once they'd dropped her off they sailed to Constantinople (modern-day Istanbul), then travelled overland back to Venice. They'd been away for 24 years.

THE TRAVELS OF MARCO POLO

In 1299, Marco Polo became a prisoner of war in Genoa. He told the story of his travels to a fellow prisoner, a writer called Rustichello, who wrote it all down. The book, which became known as *The Travels of Marco Polo*, included fantastic descriptions of Kublai Khan's palace (covered in gold and silver and big enough to have 6,000 people for dinner), and Chinese inventions such as gunpowder, paper money, silk and porcelain. Polo's adventures in China became famous and inspired other explorers, including Christopher Columbus. Marco Polo and his father and uncle never went back to China.

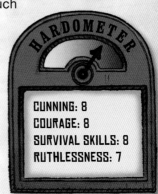

HARDOMETER

CUNNING: 8
COURAGE: 8
SURVIVAL SKILLS: 8
RUTHLESSNESS: 7

MUNGO PARK

Mungo Park was a Scottish doctor who explored western Africa, but didn't live to tell the tale.

HARD NUT RATING: 6

INTERIOR AFRICA

Mungo Park trained as a doctor but wanted to be an explorer. He met a famous botanist called James Banks, who'd travelled with Captain Cook and was president of the Association for Promoting the Discovery of the Interior Parts of Africa – exactly what Park was interested in. In 1795, the Association sent Park to western Africa to explore the River Niger.

IMPRISONED IN AFRICA

The slave trade was still legal in Britain at the time, and Park's companions on the trip included Johnson, an ex-slave, and Demba, a slave who'd been promised his freedom after the expedition. Park wore unsuitable European clothes for exploring, and kept his notes under his tall hat. Curious Bondou tribespeople made him hand over his umbrella and his coat, but far worse was to come: Park was taken prisoner by the Emir of Ludamar, and poor Demba was taken away and sold. After four months Park managed to escape, helped by Johnson, and continued his expedition: he reached the River Niger and followed it for 120 kilometres, before making his way to the coast to return to England.

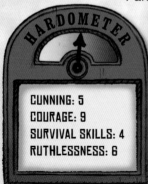

HARDOMETER

CUNNING: 5
COURAGE: 9
SURVIVAL SKILLS: 4
RUTHLESSNESS: 6

AFRICAN ADVENTURE

Park's ordeal didn't put him off, and in 1805 he began a second expedition to Africa with a team of around 40 people. But very unwisely, they set off in the rainy season. Everyone in the team got sick, they were attacked by bandits, and the guide was nearly eaten by a crocodile. The expedition had left Portsmouth in January 1805 – when they reached the River Niger in the middle of August, only 11 of them were still alive. Three months later only five were left.

MYSTERIOUS DISAPPEARANCE

Park and his four companions set off down the River Niger by canoe, but they never returned. Exactly what happened remains a mystery, but they were probably killed by hostile tribespeople. Park's body was never found. Over 20 years after his disappearance, his son Thomas went in search of his father. Sadly, he died of a fever before he'd got very far.

NEIL ARMSTRONG

Armstrong's amazing journey into the unknown didn't take him across seas, mountains, deserts or icy waters, but into space.

HARD NUT
RATING: 8.5

SPACE RACE

By the time Neil Armstrong was born in Ohio, USA, in 1930, most places on Earth had been explored. Space, on the other hand, was still a mystery. Yuri Gagarin of the USSR became the first person to travel into space in 1961. After that, the USSR and the USA, the two biggest world powers at the time, raced each other to land people on the Moon.

ASTRONAUTS WANTED

Armstrong earned his pilot's license when he was just 16, then studied aeronautical engineering at university. His studies were interrupted by the Korean War, where Armstrong flew fighter planes for the USA. Once he'd finished his education, he went to work as a test pilot for America's space organisation, NASA. He flew supersonic aircraft, including the 4000-mph X-15, as well as rockets, helicopters and gliders. In 1962 he was chosen for the USA's astronaut programme – he was on his way to the Moon.

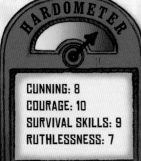

HARDOMETER

CUNNING: 8
COURAGE: 10
SURVIVAL SKILLS: 9
RUTHLESSNESS: 7

ONE SMALL STEP

America's Apollo 11 mission blasted off on 16 July 1968. Three men made up the moon-bound team: Buzz Aldrin, Michael Collins and the commander, Neil Armstrong. Just like explorers hundreds of years before them, they were setting out into uncharted territory, with no back-up plan if things went wrong. On 21 July, Armstrong landed the lunar module, *Eagle*, and became the first person to set foot on the surface of the Moon, followed by Buzz Aldrin. They collected samples from the Moon's surface, and set up a mirror to help astronomers on Earth record the Moon's position.

MOON MAN

Armstrong instantly became one of the most famous people on Earth, and his words when he was about to step onto the Moon – "One small step for a man, one giant leap for mankind" – became some of the most quoted ever. He never flew into space again, but worked for NASA and as a professor of engineering. He died in 2012.

SPACE TRAVEL

Neil Armstrong (see page 42) and his team are some of the most famous people who've been brave enough to travel into space. But there are other space pioneers . . .

YURI GAGARIN

Gagarin, from the USSR (which is now Russia and other countries) blasted into space in 1961 and became the first ever person in space. He orbited the Earth in his spacecraft in 89 minutes and 34 seconds.

VALENTINA TERESHKOVA

In 1963, Tereshkova (also from the USSR) became the first woman in space. The following year she had a baby – the first person to be born whose parents had both travelled into space (Tereshkova's husband was a cosmonaut).

ALEXEI LEONOV

Leonov (from the USSR again) was the first person to space walk. In 1965, he left his spacecraft and stayed outside, attached by a tether, for over twelve minutes. His spacesuit had inflated while he was in space, and he only just managed to get back inside the spacecraft by opening a valve in his suit to deflate it.

SPACE ANIMALS

The first creature from Earth in space wasn't human: fruit flies were sent into space first! In 1957 Laika the dog became the first animal to orbit the Earth. Other animals in space include tortoises, worms, monkeys, butterflies, bees, spiders and jellyfish!

LIVING IN SPACE

Some people have lived in space for months on end
(on space stations) but living in space has its difficulties.
Here are a few of them:

- Space sickness – just like any other kind of travel
  sickness – is a common problem.

- Astronauts have to be strapped into bed to go to sleep,
  and they have to get used to not having night-time
  and daytime.

- Washing is a problem, because liquids form droplets and
  float about. So astronauts use soap that can be used
  without water.

- Zero gravity means that people don't use their muscles
  as much – they have to use exercise machines to keep
  in shape.

- Space food has to be lightweight and easy to store, so
  it's often freeze-dried, which isn't always very appetising.
  And astronauts have to be careful not to make crumbs
  that can float about and clog up their instruments.

PONCE DE LEON

Spanish explorer Ponce de Leon searched for the fountain of youth, founded the first settlement in Puerto Rico, and discovered Florida.

HARD NUT RATING: 9

GOVERNING HISPANIOLA

We don't know for sure, but Juan Ponce de Leon might have begun his exploring career with Christopher Columbus (see page 10) as part of Columbus's second expedition to the New World in 1493. We do know that by 1502 Ponce de Leon was a captain in the West Indies, working for the governor of Hispaniola (the second biggest island in the West Indies, now divided into Haiti and the Dominican Republic). Ponce de Leon ruthlessly put a stop to a native Indian mutiny, and was made governor of the eastern part of the island as a reward.

GOING FOR GOLD

Ponce de Leon wasn't just ruthless, he was greedy too. He'd heard reports of gold on the neighbouring island of Puerto Rico, so in 1508 he set off to explore it. He founded Caparra, the oldest colonial settlement on the island, and became Puerto Rico's governor for a while, until rivals kicked him out.

MAGIC FOUNTAIN

Ponce de Leon heard reports of a fountain of eternal youth – whoever drank from it would become younger – on a mythical island called Bimini. He set off from Puerto Rico in 1513 and landed on the coast of Florida (which he named), close to the modern city of St Augustine. He didn't realise he wasn't on an island, but on the edge of an absolutely enormous continent. He sailed south through the Florida Keys chain of islands, and landed further south on Florida's coast, but he still hadn't found the magic fountain. Which isn't all that surprising. No one's sure whether Ponce de Leon really believed in it.

CONQUERING

Ponce de Leon headed back to Spain, where he was made the governor of Florida and Bimini, then sailed all the way back to Florida again, in 1521, to do a bit of colonising and conquering. But Ponce de Leon was thwarted – hostile Indians attacked, and he was wounded by one of their arrows. He made it to Cuba, but died there soon after.

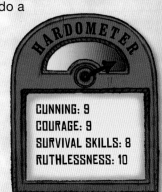

HARDOMETER

CUNNING: 9
COURAGE: 9
SURVIVAL SKILLS: 8
RUTHLESSNESS: 10

VASCO DA GAMA

HARD NUT RATING: 9

Portuguese explorer Vasco da Gama sailed around the tip of Africa and opened a new sea route from Europe to the East.

AROUND AFRICA

While Vasco da Gama was growing up, Portuguese explorers were sailing further and further down the western coast of Africa searching for a sea route to India. In 1488 Bartolomeu Dias reached the tip of Africa – the Cape of Good Hope – but didn't go any further because his crew were too frightened of sea monsters and other perils. King Manuel I of Portugal chose Vasco da Gama to sail around the Cape of Good Hope all the way to India.

EAST TO INDIA

In 1497 Vasco da Gama set sail from Lisbon with a fleet of four ships. He rounded the Cape of Good Hope and sailed across to India, arriving in Calicut (modern-day Kozhikode) in May 1498. The Hindu ruler was suspicious of the Europeans, but da Gama managed to load his ships with spices and jewels for his return trip to Portugal, which had to sail in the face of monsoon winds. When they finally arrived back in Portugal, two years after they'd set out, only two of the ships were left, and just 55 of the 170 crew (many of them had died from scurvy).

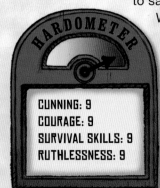

HARDOMETER

CUNNING: 9
COURAGE: 9
SURVIVAL SKILLS: 9
RUTHLESSNESS: 9

SPICE ROUTE

Despite the losses, the King of Portugal was overjoyed with Vasco da Gama and rewarded him for his hard work: the new sea route could be used to trade in valuable eastern spices and jewels, and was a lot easier than lugging everything overland, which meant a huge money-making opportunity for Portugal. In 1502, da Gama set off on a second trip, aiming to grab trade routes from the Arabs, and make everyone along the way swear loyalty to the King of Portugal. His methods were ruthless: one story says that he seized the cargo of a captured ship, then set fire to it with hundreds of passengers on board.

VICEROY OF INDIA

In the following years, Vasco da Gama's trade route made Portugal wealthy. In 1524 he was made Viceroy of India, but he fell ill and died within a few months of arriving there.

MARY KINGSLEY

Mary Kingsley was a Victorian lady with a taste for adventure that took her all the way to Africa.

HARD NUT
RATING: 6.8

ADVENTURE BECKONS

Mary Kingsley's father was a doctor who travelled to the South Seas, the United States and Africa. When he came home he told stories of his adventures. Mary stayed at home and looked after her sick mother and her brother, but yearned to travel. She had to wait until she was 30 before she could do anything about her plans. Both her parents had died, and they'd left enough money for Mary to live comfortably without having to work. But Mary didn't want to live comfortably: she wanted to go to Africa.

EXPLORING AFRICA

On her first African adventure, Kingsley sailed to the Canary Islands, then on to Sierra Leone and Angola in West Africa, where she spent a few months living with local people and finding out about African life. The following year, 1893, she was back. This time she visited the West African country of Gabon, where she canoed up the Ogooué River, and met the Fang people, who were said to be cannibals. She became an expert on African insects, and collected insects, fish and plants for the British Museum as she travelled. She found several unrecorded species of fish, three of which were named after her. She also climbed the 4,000 metre Mount Cameroon, the first European woman to make the climb, via a route that no other European had attempted.

ALARMING TALES

When she got back to England Kingsley wrote a book, *Travels in West Africa*, which became a bestseller. She also gave readings and lectures, including many alarming stories: she spoke of how she drove away an attacking leopard by throwing a jug at it, and hit a crocodile on the head with her paddle as it tried to climb into her canoe. Kingsley returned to Africa in 1899 to work as a nurse in the Boer War, where she caught typhoid and died.

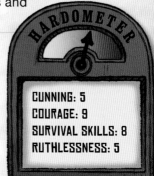

HARDOMETER

CUNNING: 5
COURAGE: 9
SURVIVAL SKILLS: 8
RUTHLESSNESS: 5

SCOTT OF THE ANTARCTIC

Scott led expeditions to one of the most perilous places on Earth – the freezing South Pole.

ANTARCTIC ADVENTURE

Robert Falcon Scott joined the British navy when he was 13, in 1871. Thirty years later, now an experienced sailor and a captain in the navy, he was chosen to lead an expedition to the Antarctic. He had never done any exploring before, but in 1901 he set off in command of the ship, *Discovery*. The expedition lasted three years, and reached further south than anyone had before. The team returned to Britain as heroes.

ROALD WAS HERE

JOURNEY TO THE POLE

Despite the harsh conditions of the Antarctic, Scott was determined to return and be the first to reach the South Pole. In 1911 he arrived on the frozen continent, leading a team of 12 men, and set off across the ice. Things began badly and got worse: many of the team's ponies died, and the dog teams turned back six months into the expedition, leaving five men to continue to the Pole. Scott and the others battled through terrible weather, dragging their own equipment with them. They finally reached the South Pole, but discovered that Roald Amundsen (see page 8) and his team had beaten them to it by a month.

ICY DEATHS

Wearily, Scott and his small team began their 1,500 kilometre journey back across the ice. The first to die was a man named Evans – he fell into a crevasse and hit his head. Another member of the team, Oates, had frostbite, and sacrificed himself by walking out into the snow, rather than delay the others. Sadly, it made no difference: Scott and the remaining two men, Wilson and Bowers, died in their tent of starvation and exposure, just 20 kilometres away from supplies that might have saved them.

SNOWY TOMB

Eight months later, a search party found the bodies of the men and Scott's diary, which recorded their last journey. Scott, Wilson and Bowers were buried under their tent, and their grave was marked by a snow cairn. In Britain, they were remembered as national heroes.

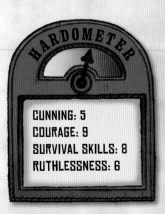

HARDOMETER

CUNNING: 5
COURAGE: 9
SURVIVAL SKILLS: 8
RUTHLESSNESS: 6

ZHENG HE

Zheng He travelled to Africa and India, expanding China's horizons further than ever before.

NORTHERN TRIBES

Zheng He was born around 1371 in the mountainous Chinese province of Yunnan. When he was about 11, Yunnan was invaded by the mighty Ming dynasty, and Zheng He was captured and sent to serve Prince Zhu Di. Hostile northern tribes were always attacking Prince Zhu Di's lands, and so Zheng He was constantly fighting them. He proved himself to be as hard as nails, and became one of the prince's chief advisers.

OVERTHROWING THE EMPEROR

Prince Zhu Di wanted to be emperor. And when the old emperor died and Zhu Di's nephew took his place, he decided to do something about it. In 1402, with Zheng He as one of his chief commanders, he marched on the Chinese imperial capital and overthrew the emperor. Now that Zhu Di was the new emperor, Zheng He was promoted to a top job, and his exploring career could begin.

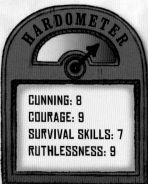

HARDOMETER

CUNNING: 8
COURAGE: 9
SURVIVAL SKILLS: 7
RUTHLESSNESS: 9

EXPLORING THE WORLD

Zheng He began the first of seven voyages in 1405. He set off in style, with maybe as many as 400 ships and more than 28,000 men. If that wasn't impressive enough, Zheng He himself was said to be more than two metres tall, with a face as broad as a tiger's and eyebrows like swords: a man you wouldn't forget. His mission was to tell everyone how powerful and wonderful China was, as well as finding out about the countries he visited, and making valuable trade routes. Altogether, he travelled around 50,000 kilometres, and visited India, Southeast Asia, Arabia and East Africa, defeating pirates and anyone else brave enough to stand up to him on the way. He brought back lots of gifts of ivory, ostriches, zebras and a giraffe, which the Chinese believed to be a mythical creature.

BURIED AT SEA

Zheng He probably died on his last voyage, in 1433. After his death, a new Ming emperor closed China to trade and even banned the building of sea-going ships. Zheng He was forgotten about for centuries, but now his intrepid explorations are famous.

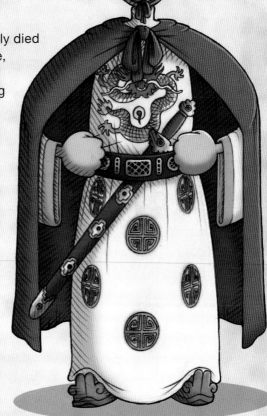

SIR WALTER RALEIGH

Walter Raleigh was an Elizabethan explorer who searched the New World for a fabled city of gold.

HARD NUT
RATING: 7

EXPLORING AMERICA

Raleigh was born around 1554 in England. He went to Oxford University and studied law in London, then got involved in wars and revolts. But his first exploring experience came in 1578 when he sailed to America with his brother-in-law.

IRELAND, POTATOES AND TOBACCO

Raleigh helped stop a rebellion in Ireland in 1580, making him one of Queen Elizabeth I's favourite young men. Later he helped defeat the Spanish Armada, and she liked him even more. The Queen made Raleigh Captain of the Guard, gave him lots of land in Ireland, and he became a politician. But in the meantime, Raleigh went back to America and tried (but failed) to found colonies. He's famous for bringing potatoes and tobacco back to Britain from his travels, but in fact the Spanish had already beaten him to it. He is probably responsible for making smoking popular, though, and there's a story that someone threw a bucket of water over him thinking he was on fire, when in fact he was having a puff on his pipe.

HARDOMETER

CUNNING: 6
COURAGE: 8
SURVIVAL SKILLS: 7
RUTHLESSNESS: 7

THE SEARCH FOR EL DORADO

In 1592 Raleigh got married, and Queen Elizabeth was so upset that she threw Raleigh and his wife into the Tower of London, and didn't let them out until 1594.

To try and get back into her good books, Raleigh set off on a voyage to find El Dorado, the fabled city of gold located somewhere in the New World. He travelled up the Orinoco River in South America, but didn't find it.

EL DORADO AGAIN

When Queen Elizabeth died, the new King James I didn't like Raleigh, and threw him into prison for 12 years. Then he sent him to have another look for El Dorado, hoping to make Britain rich. When Raleigh didn't find the golden city, King James had him beheaded. Raleigh's wife kept his embalmed head in a bag until she died, when the head was finally buried.

HARD NUT TRAVELLERS AND EXPLORERS TIMELINE

C. 970

Leif Ericson, the Viking explorer who sailed to North America, was born. He didn't stay in America, but was probably the first European to ever go there.

1324

Marco Polo, who had travelled to China and lived there for 24 years, died in Venice.

1405

Chinese explorer Zhen He set off on his first voyage. He travelled to Asia, Africa, the Middle East and India.

1492

Christopher Columbus made his first voyage across the Atlantic to the West Indies.

1497

Vasco da Gama set sail on his journey around Africa to India, opening up a new trade route for Portugal.

1519

Ferdinand Magellan set off on the first ever round-the-world trip. He was killed in the Philippines before his ships completed the voyage.

1521

Ponce de Leon, the first European discoverer of Florida, died. He tried and failed to find the Fountain of Youth.

1547

Hernan Cortes died, having conquered and ruled the Aztec Empire in the New World.

1618

Sir Walter Raleigh, English explorer of the New World, was executed. He searched for El Dorado, the fabled city of gold.

1768

Captain Cook began his first voyage of exploration, which took him across all the world's oceans.

1795

Mungo Park set off to explore the River Niger in western Africa on his first expedition.

1803

Lewis and Clark set off on their journey from St Louis in America's Midwest to the Pacific Ocean. They arrived home more than two years later.

1813

African explorer David Livingstone was born. He lived and worked in Africa for years, and died there.

1857

Burton and Speke began their expedition to find the source of the White Nile.

1860

Burke and Wills set off on their fateful trip across Australia. They made it from the south to the north of the continent, but died before they could make the return journey.

1872

Polar explorer Roald Amundsen was born. His expedition was the first to arrive at the South Pole, beating Scott by about a month.

1892

Mary Kingsley made her first trip to Africa. She went on to climb Mount Cameroon, canoe up the Ogooue River, and become an expert on African insects.

1912

Robert Falcon Scott died on his expedition to the South Pole.

1937

Amelia Earhart went missing on her pioneering round-the-world flight. She was the first woman to cross the Atlantic by plane.

1968

Neil Armstrong became the first person to set foot on the Moon.

GLOSSARY

ABORIGINE Someone who is part of the Aboriginal race of Australia

ANTIBIOTICS Medicines that kill bacterial infections

AVIATOR Pilot of an aircraft

BESIEGED Surrounded by enemy forces

BOTANISTS Experts in plants

CIRCUMNAVIGATED Travelled all around

COLONISTS People from another country who move into a new country and take control of it

CONQUISTADOR A conqueror, especially relating to the Spanish conquerors of Mexico and Peru in the 16th century

COSMONAUT Russian name for an astronaut

CREVASSES Deep, open cracks in a glacier or ice sheet

EMBALMED When a dead body is treated with chemicals in order to preserve it

EMPIRE A group of states or countries ruled by one leader or state

ENSLAVING Forcing people to become slaves

EXPANSES Wide, open areas

GANGRENE Rotting of body tissue when wounds get infected

INDIGENOUS Native to a country

INFESTED Over-run with

INTREPID Courageous and bold

MALARIA Deadly disease carried by mosquitoes

MAROONING Abandoning on a deserted island

MONSOON Large winds that change direction each season

MUTINY Rebellion against authority

NATIVE Someone born in or associated with a specific place

NOMADS People who move from place to place

NOTORIOUS Famous for something bad

ORBITED Went around an object in space

OUTLAW Someone who is banned from their country

REBELLION Break away from (or resistance to) authority

SABRE Sword

SCURVY Deadly disease caused by a lack of vitamin C

SUPERSONIC Faster than the speed of sound

TEEMING Full of

TYPHOID Deadly disease of the digestive system

VICEROY Governor representing the King or Queen in a colony

INDEX